'We are not amused by this appalling book'

The Publishers

Spike Milligan's Transports of Delight

Photographs by Popperfoto

First published in Great Britain in 1974
Copyright © 1974 Spike Milligan
Productions Ltd (text)

© 1974 Popperfoto (photographs)
© 1974 Sidgwick & Jackson)
(design and concept)

Printed in Great Britain by
Tinlings (1973) Limited, Prescot
(a member of the Oxley Printing Group Ltd)
for Sidgwick and Jackson Limited
1 Tavistock Chambers, Bloomsbury Way
London WC1A 2SG

Sidgwick & Jackson
London

Chapter 1

THE FIRST TWO BILLION YEARS

Many many moons ago (about 6,000,000,000,000,000,0 B.C.), a hairy thing appeared in a tree by permission of God and Co. Limited; the thing was called Man. Later, another thing turned up, this was called Woman, and that's how the trouble started. However, it is not the domestic or sex life that we scan, nay, it is the way they moved themselves from one place to another. Now, if you observe the Gibbon monkey at the zoo, you will get a good idea of the first method of hairy transport; it was done by swinging from branch to branch.

But alas, Homo Sapiens (the knowing one) must have indulged himself in lots of eating, thus gaining weight and finally finding that levitation from branch to branch became more and more difficult as he put on poundage. In the end, this form of transport was terminated by (a) the branch breaking under his weight, and/or (b) missing the branch altogether. The injuries rendered during his falling phase turned his mind against this mode of locomotion, and he found it less injurious to stay on the ground. From there on he ambled about on all fours, much the same way as the modern chimpanzee. Of course, he fell prey to various animals such as the sabre-toothed Tiger, and to put as much space as possible 'twixt this carnivore and himself, he adopted two forms of safety: one was to climb back *up* the tree, the second was to try and out-run the tiger. He found his four-legged ambling gate no answer to the bounding momentum of the tiger, so, the numbers of Homo Sapiens that fell prey to animals were massive, but it kept his numbers down.

Transport: Aquatic
Two members of the Hindu Navy, using ancient Yoga method of inflating their stomachs with air thus affording them a means of escape from sinking ships.

Chapter 2
THE NEXT TWO BILLION YEARS

In Ireland, nothing had happened. During this phase Homo Sapiens would, to spot any danger, stand on his hind legs to view the surround for predators, and, of course, yes! you've guessed! he was in the process of standing upright, and thus his legs started to improve and develop along the lines of running-like-bloody-hell-from-a-Tyrannosaurus-Rex, and, brother!, that needed some running. In those days the four-minute mile was broken a dozen times a day, but we are coming to the opening of the story of transport. Man, now standing semi-right, could travel much greater distances over flat treeless country than his monkey cousins couldn't traverse, so here was the first free form of transport, 'Shanks Pony', and man was going to be stuck with that for a very long time. It would appear that it was at Olduvai Gorge, round about Two Million years ago, that this was going on.

Air Transport: Mindshrinker
BOAC show their forthcoming cheap get-there-your-bloody-self passenger service

Chapter 3

ECONOMIC CONSEQUENCES OF NEOLITHIC TRANSPORT

In Ireland, nothing happened. Man was now a mobile hunter, walking in a semi-upright position (known to parliamentarians as the Back Bencher Slouch) and was able to chase game and kill it. A new problem now beset this creature (and has a bearing on the march of transport), that was a place to live, as against trees – somewhere to keep the rain off and kip.

A Cave was the answer, and so man became a Troglodyte. The old woman and the kids stayed home while he and the lads went off on a Mammoth binge. This was a simple process, you chased one over a cliff and it killed itself. But now came the problem of lugging great hunks of Woolly Mammoth meat a mile back to the cave, let's call the man Ug . . . This Ug says, 'I'm shagged out carrying this stuff home bent double, and nearly ruptured, I can't keep it up. Next time, you (The Missus) and the kids 'ave got to come along and 'elp.' So, there we see The Wife and kids all sweating under the weight of a hundredweight of buffalo meat, while walking behind is Ug, burden free and singing a merry Neolithic tune, having invented a transport that left him unburdened. But every worm turns, and one day the missus said 'Look 'ere, me and the kids are not 'avin orl this bloody liftin' . . . if you don't stop it we're going back to my mother in that tree over there.' Checkmate.

Transport: Beach Buggy
A special riderless tricycle invented especially for pulling over pebbly
beaches: the man in this picture used to be six foot three.

Chapter 4

SOCIO-ECONOMIC ASPECTS OF LOCOMOTION

In Ireland, nothing happened. The transport problem was on! Temporary solution, he moved to the lakeside, where animals had to drink, and knocked them off there, and ate them in situ. When they moved to different grazing lands, he followed, simple, but was it? Ah ha! Man started to collect chattels, pots, pans, rock axes, spears, hides, etc., etc., and they had to be carried. Time came when the stuff was too much for the family, so Checkmate number two, but Ug comes up with a winner. Why not *drag* the stuff? This worked save that certain chattels like pottery jugs were smashed in transit, sooooo, how to drag and yet not make contact with the ground? Ug comes up again, and this time we have two poles joined by an animal hide into a sort of stretcher. One end is pulled by the Ug family, the other end trails on the ground, great success! (Red Indians used this up to 1880.) But More always leads to more. Soon the stretcher was loaded to capacity with the increasing possessions that man is wont to create; I won't say at this early stage it was the TV but most certainly there were bulky goods plus increasing numbers of squalling kids. No, Ug would have to think of something bigger, no, not bigger, bigger needed more people to haul it along, no, this would have to be something EASIER. Ug sat, stood and lay down, the word EASIER kept looming in his mind's eye, and his mind's ear.

Transport: Rare
A two-wheeled umbrella being pulled by Rhinostrihorse

Chapter 5

THE DAWN OF THE WHEEL

In Ireland, nothing happened. The next step was to be man's greatest step in the story of transport. It was, is, and always will be the greatest of man's inventions outside medical science, it was the penicillin of locomotion, and that was the wheel. We don't know the name of the man who invented it, but he was a true genius, bearing in mind that that terrible Easter two-hour traffic jam you were in was impossible without him.

Transport: Inexplainable

Rare Canadian photo. It shows two dogs wearing dark glasses on a sunless day. A third dog is wearing motoring goggles. The wheels of all the carts are in a ditch. The boy drivers all look baffled, and I'm not surprised. Any reader who can give a rational explanation to this picture is welcome to it

Chapter 6

THE DAWN OF THE HORSE

Love makes the world go round they say, however, the wheel makes it go round much quicker, so the wheel it was that would be the backbone of transport until the advent of flying. So you see, the wheel had a long way to go before it had any competition and, even then, it was still the essential ingredient of the highway. Now, I could end there, but that would be shortchanging the book, so, dear reader, let us continue. We now have man pulling rough carts with wooden wheels as he journeyed the earth. Somewhere along the line, that is, several Ugs later, Ug No. 23, who had taken the wheel for granted, found pulling the Cart very wearying. As he often said, 'I'm shagged out, if only someone else or something else would pull it for me, I'd have my hands free to do something more to my liking, like sleeping or chasing some young bulging-bosomed female from another tribe.' Eureka! galloping across Ug 23's horizon comes a delightful ungulate which would, after several modifications, become known as the Horse. It galloped here, it galloped there, it galloped up hills, it galloped down hills, it was capable, as Ug 23 adjudicated, of galloping anywhere, and as there was plenty of anywhere in those days, it seemed a good idea to catch this wild creature and see if it could be taught to gallop in all directions (a) with a family of ten on its back or (b) pulling the family cart. (a) was a disaster, the horse collapsed, but (b) showed promise. By clubbing the bucking whinnying kicking tornado, they tranquillized it into standing still. Then, using flaxen ropes and various tying devices, they hitched it to the cart. When the horse regained its compus, it set off at a terrorfying speed across the land. They never saw it again.

Transport: River
A man training a tame wartime naval torpedo for peacetime river travel

Transport: Chinese
Early Chinese Royal Air Force Sailborne Bombers, about to take off to bomb the Japanese

Transport: Philippines
Palanquins for carrying people with curvature of the spine

Chapter 7

THE AGE OF REVOLUTION

In Ireland, nothing happened. Next time, thought Ug 23, we must all get *in* the cart and go *with* it, that way they would get information as to how the horse behaved in relationship to the cart. And so it came to pass that a second horse was clubbed to a standstill, the cart loaded, and in a few minutes they were all hanging on for dear life screaming to get off as the latest form of locomotion galloped across the English landscape. All the chattels were lost, but the family remained intact, the horse died and the cart fell to pieces. It was a lesson, but about what, no one was sure. IDEA! The cart would have to be heavier to slow the creature down, so the whole thing started again. They built a giant wooden cart, tied boulders underneath to act as an early type of suppressor, 'tranquillized' the beast and waited for it to wear off, and off they went, but this time at a much more respectable pace. 'We've got the measure of this bastard,' said Ug 23, and he had. Man had his very first animal slave, but the trouble now was to stop members of the family trying to eat it. These were lean times, and the horse was a cert for the Sunday joint, so now a guard had to be set over it all night. This was by way of being the first 'Insurance' policy that was to plague all people with means of private travel. With the horse we have to lump the Yak, the Camel, the Buffalo, the Donkey, even the Dog. So now man had four-legged power, was he satisfied? Not really, I mean, how do you get a horse to gallop the straights of Dover? Not on, so now we have Ug 75 standing at a great water and saying, 'How am I going to get the family across this lot?' Now we, in our wisdom, know that the answer to water is a boat. To Ug 75 this vision did not occur.

Transport: Thailand? Buffalo

Ba tuk Su, a Thai Navy Captain, using a water buffalo to represent the
Thai Navy while he waits for a battle ship to be built

Chapter 8

THE HISTORY OF NAVIGATION (PART 1)

N o one is positive when man became nautical. There is evidence of water travel on Prehistoric lakes in Poland, so somewhere about 20,000 B.C. I suspect that Ug 97 came by a boat, first by falling into the water and hanging on to a log, then sitting astride, then making outriggers of smaller logs. My own personal opinion of how it went was something like this: a pleasant day in summer, young son Ug 97 is knapping a stone axe, mother comes running in:

Mother: Son, Son, your father wants you to invent a boat.
Son: Where is he?
Mother: In the middle of the lake . . . drowning.

May be a bit far out but a good basis for a feasibility study.

Transport: Anti-reproduction
A machine for keeping the population down. When the husband and wife
feel like it, they all get on the bike and drive away instead

Chapter 9

THE HISTORY OF NAVIGATION (PART 2)

In Ireland, nothing was happening, but they were working at it. After the wheel, the boat/ship/canoe/raft was the greatest step in the history of transport. From now on waterways became open, and with them the first tentative steps towards travel between different lands and nations.

Transport: Wooden
A bullock-drawn portable four-wheeled bath used by Indian mystics on their
way to the office – the umbrella is to prevent bath water escaping upwards

Chapter 10

TRANSPORT IN THE AGE OF NEBUCHADNEZZAR

ll this was an incredible jump in thinking from that beetle-browed thing called Homo Erectus who was walking around scratching his arse and eating ants about a million and a half years ago; it is also incredible that he had absolutely no outside stimulii, it was all his own work. This was, of course, the pattern that was leading him away from the primitive world of the animal and emerging as the greatest thinking creature on earth, possibly the Universe, but also the greatest disaster, and the worst is yet to come. By now, other animals around the globe were in his employ: the Ass, the Lllama, the Camel, the Ox, all these he had also learned to ride, he could also ride a Horse. So we now had The Wheeled Cart, the animals to pull it, and the Boat. These three were to be the main stay of man's efforts at conveyance. Of course, it had many variations added to this – the Oxen that was domesticated and put to the Plough – and that was the pattern for the next hundreds of years. There were variations from two-wheel and four-wheel carts, chariots, the last mentioned was possibly the first use of peaceful-oriented invention being put to military use. There were hundreds of variants of the wheeled transport of the time, varying from heavy predecessors of the Sussex Hay Waggon, found in Central European countries, to delicate four-wheeled ritual chieftain carts in Nordic climes.

Transport: Balloon
A three-man balloon starts from Marble Arch. It goes via Switzerland to
Finchley to avoid the rush hour on the Northern Line

Transport : Horsedrawn
A brilliant invention, a motorless charabanc, giving all the comforts of
motor transport at a fraction of the cost – by starving the horses

Transport: Hygienic
A portable Gents Toilet for use by busy business men on their way to work

Chapter 11

FROM TUTANKHAMEN TO POPE JULIUS II

 **W**e are now somewhere in the early kingdom period of the Egyptian people. Let us suppose that it was in countries in the Bible Belt that got going first that the refinements were going on. The military were now using mounted troops to beat the hell out of each other, which were the direct linear predecessors to the Panzers of the Third Reich, so man has now absorbed transport methods into destruction patterns. We have to make a great leap forward in time to what were the next important transitions in the development in transport.

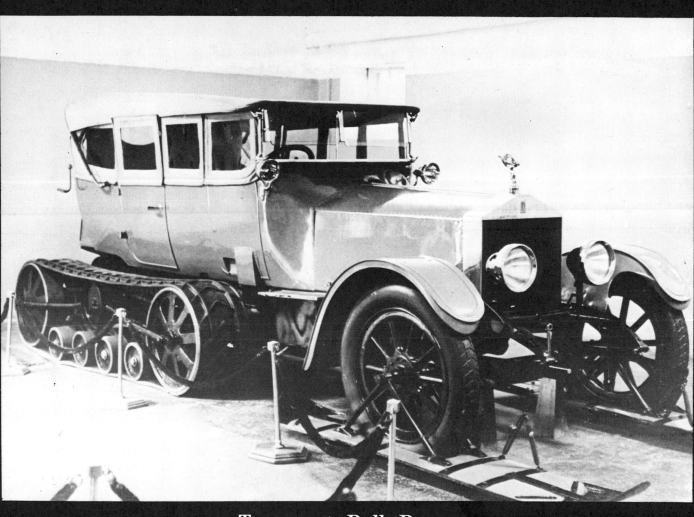

Transport: Rolls Royce
A modified Rolls Royce owned by the Director of Bertorellis for driving over Ice Cream

Chapter 12

Aspects of Renascence Transport

In Ireland, nothing had happened. During the Renascence (Italian) there were many inventions on paper that were incredibly ahead of their time. One of the front runners, Leonardo da Vinci: his drawings and models of aeroplanes were practical, and launched from his window glided to the ground safely where the enraged natives burnt them, and knowing the fate of Galileo, he refrained from going further, and concentrated on the Mona Lisa. Fancy, had he been given his head, we might have had the six-seater flying Mona Lisa. 'Hello, good morning, Italia Airlines welcomes you aboard. This is your captain Leonardo da Vinci speaking. You are now flying in the most beautiful aircraft in the world, powered by two Michael Angelo Slaves.'

'Stop this book, I want to get out'

Transport: Double Elephant
A number 139A going from Poona Cantonment to the Empire Bioscope to
see the original silent version of Beau Geste with Ronald Colman. Note Gary
Cooper dressed as Legionnaire at top window, awaiting the sound version

Transport: World War 2
A crowd of commissioned bloody fools who don't know that to ride a bike
you get on it

Chapter 13

THE HISTORY OF NAVIGATION (PART 3)

Boats had become ships that could traverse all the known waters of this earth, they would and were opening up trade and at the same time destroying primitive cultures, some of great beauty, witness the Conquistadores. Now *there* was a crowd of bastards for you, I think they called it Christianity. By way of reference, the Mayas, Aztecs, etc. had never seen a horse prior to the invasion, and even stranger, the Indian of America never used it to an advantage until the Conflict in North America between himself and the Settlers, when he became a magnificent horseman using tricks that no riding academy had dreamed of, but more of that later.

Transport: Pygmy Power
Pygmy chieftain practising for a bus strike in the Congo

Chapter 14

THE DAWN OF THE CANAL

Meantime, in Ireland nothing had happened. An early inland highway existed in Egyptian, Greek and Roman times – this was the Canal. It fell into obscurity but was revived in the eighteenth century, for the industrial revolution. The Canal was, I suppose, really railways on water. Loaded barges pulled by our dear old friend the horse, were plying up and down the country. It was transport on a bulk scale, carrying much more goods per one horse than on land. It was a good thing for man, who was on his way to over-population and had to start transporting large amounts of all goods. If only they had been carrying contraceptives, London might still be a series of small villages and more of us might be sane, but time was marching on and a new world-shaking invention was at hand, that was man-made artificial energy. It was to create a Transport Boom that exploded in all directions. It happened two-fold: Steam and Petrol. Steam was the first to come into service.

Transport: Siberian Air Lines
This aeroplane travelled some 5,789 miles and still hasn't taken off – hence
the disturbed look of the passengers who only wanted to travel thirty miles

Transport: Immoral
Young Almees of the Ouled Nail tribe of Algeria, travelling from their
village in the Aures Mountains to a town, in the hope of earning, through
immorality, a dowry sufficient to enable them to return home, resume the
veil, and settle down to married life in their mountain homes

Transport: Gastronomic
A Chinese restaurant on its way to London

Chapter 15

THE ROMANCE OF STEAM

The Scene, a Humble Scots family hoose. A Kettle steams on the Hob, a Humble Scots lad by the name of James watches the steam issuing from the blackened spout. Suddenly he leaps up: 'Mither, Mither,' he says in fluent Scots, 'I've just invented steam,' and by god he had, he must have immediately taken out a Patent.

Patent Officer: Now boy, what have you got wrapped in that strange parcel?
Watt: Sir, I canna tell a lie, it's my new invention, Steam.
Officer: Steam?
Watt: Steam, Surr.
Officer: How do you spell it?

Watt: I don't.
Officer: Don't?
Watt: Once I spell it, the secret will be out. No, for the time I will call it a Railway Booking Office, for sure as night follows day, that's what my invention will lead to.

Watt didn't know it, but he was inventing British Railways, and lateness.

A man called Stephenson captured some of James Watt's steam, inserted it into a boiler on wheels and it started going round the room.

Patent Officer: What have you got in that large Brown Paper parcel?
Stephenson: I cannot tell you, if I did the secret would be out, no, I will call it a Rocket.

Transport: Bicycle
Lord Nuffield at high speed on a Bone Shaker. It displaced so many of his bones that he was forced to invent the Morris Motor to save his life

Chapter 16

THE SPACE AGE

The rest is history. The Rocket was the name of the first steam train, the first thing to oust muscle power as a mode of propulsion. It was as fantastic a success as the horse, in fact, from now on, the horse was to gradually drop out of transport and revert to eating grass, throwing little girls and appearing on Television. The horse had had its day, 'Thank God' said saddle-sore Ug 98675643. With this new power, expansion of territory, and business, leisure was to become limitless. Railways started to make unknown areas accessible in conditions of comparative comfort, that is if you travelled first class, if not you sat in an open carriage at the back dying of smoke, asphyxia and voting Labour. Every boy wanted to be a Steam Train Driver.

Transport: Holiday
A tricycle made for showing ladies' knickers

Transport: Aerial
A man travelling by empty talk bubbles

Transport: Hong Kong
Two coolies carrying a table that was shot by an antique dealer at an auction

Chapter 17

THE DECLINE OF THE CANAL

In Ireland, nothing was happening. Soon the landscape was criss-crossed with the iron way. In North America, its thundering wheels spelled the end of the North American Indians' way of life. From carriage windows 'Sportsmen' blasted at the defenceless bison, and slaughtered them in their thousands. For years afterwards their bones bleached in the sun and became known as the Great White way and, later, Broadway. This new devastating form of transportation had the same effect on the public mind as us in relationship to the first men on the moon and this was only a little over a hundred and thirty odd years ago. This was only the beginning. There, thundering down the corridors of time was, wait for it . . . THE PETROL ENGINE! (run for the hills, folks) . . .

Transport: India
Elephants taking the Taj Mahal for a walk

Transport: Canine, Holland 1930
A Dutch maid delivering dogs' milk on a wooden cart

Transport: Double Oxen
An English sherry shipper in his HP ox cart waiting for the wheels to arrive

Chapter 18
THE DECLINE OF THE HORSE

Now, we don't know whether we are as in love with the last-named invention as we first thought we were. This little monster was the penultimate creation of combustible energy. From it, in exchange for liberating our legs from the drudgery of walking, it filled our lungs with carbon monoxide, not a very good swap. Off shoots of this came: the Motor Cycle, the Speed Boat, for a while we had the Electrified Tram and Trolley Buss, and, looming large, the prospect of Sky Travel. The Wright brothers set it up and it flew, and now the three main dimensions of physical space had been conquered; the casualties were the horse, the canal barge, and most farm beasts of burden. The great pattern of transport as we know it today was soon to evolve. Air Travel became the quickest, and therefore with an expanding economy it went further ahead of its rival the railway. One imagined that with giant planes like the Canopus Flying Boat, and Imperial Airways flying from London to Australia with a dining room, lounge and bedroom for passengers, that little more could be added, but come the War, men on all sides are racking their brains for a method of propulsion that will shoot the enemy bombers from the skies, and by crikey it was the baddies who did it. Messerschmidt turns up with a devastating new engine that develops 1,980 static thrust that runs rings round allied fighters and bombers in the dying days of the war, mind you Frank Whittle had invented one earlier, but the Germans got into action with it first, and were faster. Who ever the which or who (Pardon?) the Jet engine swept before it in the Transport field, it could get man from London to Australia on an ordinary passenger flight in thirty-four odd hours, mind you, you got aboard in London in the prime of health smiling clean-shaven and fresh, and then debussed at Sydney a broken-down unshaven premature wreck red-eyed and alcoholic and unaware what the time of the day was. Travel was getting faster, but much

Transport: Early Egyptian
A petrol-operated donkey cart

less comfortable, and in the case I've just mentioned, one needed twenty-four hours' sleep or a brain operation to recover. Jet travel hasn't ended there, a new Stratospheric monster is with us, the Concorde. With this you can breakfast in London and have dinner in Australia, which no doubt the traveller will immediately throw up. With all this, one would think we'd got it made but, no, none of these engines could take us to the moon. And so we come to the latest and most formidable machines made by man, the Lunar Space rocket, using thrust on a massive scale to release it from the earth's gravitational field. It has done the journey a dozen times with success, even as I write this an unmanned space ship is about to go into orbit around the sun, it suddenly seems as if we are all just starting again, I think I'll go out for a walk.

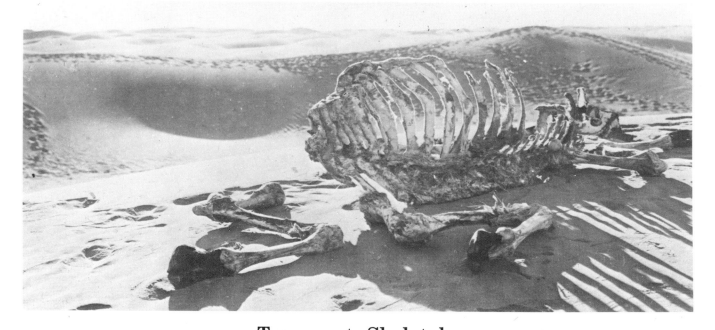

Transport: Skeletal
The skeleton of a dead E-Type Jaguar which died from a surfeit of Mechanics

Transport: When it becomes Lunatic

These are two sailors on board a giant oil tanker. To get from one end to the other on time, they have to use bicycles. They are building bigger tankers. The largest is being built in Japan: the Captain is to have a Mini Minor to drive about from one end to the other

Chapter 19

MY LIFE IN TRANSPORT

I myself was the most fortunate of little boys, fate was to decree it that I would enjoy the whole concourse of travel, in the exact chronological order that man had invented it in. I was born in India, the reason being that both my parents were there, in India, in 1923. The motor car was a rarity, all the military transport was horse-drawn, as were the guns of my father's regiment, the Royal Artillery. So, I walked as a little boy, then I rode a horse (See Picture). I then travelled by Bullock Cart, I include a photo (very faded) of one taken by me during

a Peacock shoot at Patas in India. My mother (right of picture) and I travelled over ten miles in that cart and the smell still adheres to me, on hot summer days my wife still puts me in the garden. I later travelled by Tonga, and the Landau, in India called the Victoria after the late Queen, I don't know why she was late, she had plenty of watches. I was forbidden by my grandmother to sit next to the native driver 'In case I caught it', she was referring to his colour. Of course, I finally borrowed my Uncle Hughie's bike, and drove it straight into the Bund river. I was so enthralled with the machine that I continued pedalling even as I disappeared below the

surface where suddenly I had a sudden desire to learn swimming. My travel chronology was running parallel with Ug's. The next photograph shows me and my parents standing by a T-model Ford, it wasn't ours, but my father was determined that we should be seen photographed with the thing. For this we waited until the owner parked it by the house, father and mother then pushed it off the road so, as father said, 'To give it a Jungle setting', the idea was to send the photo home to his impoverished mother and father to show how well he was doing, so well in fact he could go on hunting trips in his own private car, which explains why my father is carrying a rifle.

Transport: China
Young boys saving shoe leather and training to be giants

Transport: Korean 1879
Early Korean Kamikazi pilot about to be launched over a cliff for his emperor

Chapter 20
THE CHALLENGE OF THE FUTURE

n 1925, I flew! Once a year Bristol Fighters of the R.A.F. stationed at Ouned Camp outside Poona would land on Poona Racecourse, and 'good little boys' were given a ride, and so I qualified. It was a dream realized. 'I'm going to go into a dive now', said the pilot, and down we raced, pulling out at the last minute. 'I bet fifty per cent of the people down there thought we were going to have an accident', he chortled. I daren't tell him that fifty per cent of the people in the plane had! So at the tender age of seven I had covered all the forms of transport that it had taken Ug ten thousand years. It didn't seem fair.

Transport: Gigantic
A huge floating thing on its way to insanity

Transport: Yak
Harrods overseas furniture removals in Lapland

Transport: Arabian style
This man is Mugagi Rhashid Muk; he is riding the camel in the economy
position. In 1923, the back of a camel was assessed for transport tax:
at the front it was three drachmas, at the back one drachma. This man
is saving two drachmas and giving himself piles

APPENDIX 1

THE HUMAN RACE MY PART IN ITS SURVIVAL

SOME SUGGESTIONS FOR ALTERNATIVE MODES OF TRANSPORT

This man is ordered to
walk in front of you to enforce
4 miles speed per hour

APPENDIX 2
TRANSPORT IN WORLD HISTORY

APPENDIX 3
THE FUTURE OF TRANSPORT